TELL ME WHY, TELL ME HOW

WHY IS THE SKY BLUE?

WIL MARA

 Marshall Cavendish
Benchmark
New York

Marshall Cavendish Benchmark
99 White Plains Road
Tarrytown, New York 10591-9001
www.marshallcavendish.us

Editor: D. Sanders
Editorial Director: Michelle Bisson
Art Director: Anahid Hamparian
Series Designer: Alex Ferrari

Library of Congress Cataloging-in-Publication Data

Mara, Wil.
Why is the sky blue? / by Wil Mara.
p. cm. — (Tell me why, tell me how)
Summary: "An examination of the phenomena and scientific principles behind why the sky appears blue"—Provided by publisher.
Includes bibliographical references and index.
ISBN-13: 978-0-7614-2108-5
ISBN-10: 0-7614-2108-4
1. Colors—Juvenile literature. 2. Rainbow—Juvenile literature. I. Title. II. Series.

QC495.5.M367 2006
535.6—dc22

2005016477

Photo research by Candlepants Incorporated

Cover photo: Julie Habel/Corbis

The photographs in this book are used by permission and through the courtesy of: *Getty Images:* Tony Hutchings, 1; Ver Jim Barber, 17. *Peter Arnold Inc.:* K. Shindel/UNEP, 4. *Photo Researchers Inc.:* Lynwood M. Chase, 5; Richard Hutchings, 6; NASA, 12; James Stevenson, 19. *Corbis:* Phil Banko, 7; John McAnulty, 8; Joson/zefa, 9; Dennis Cooper/zefa, 14; Frithjof Hiirdes/zefa, 16; Warren Faidley, 15; Jim Zuckerman, 18; Bettmann, 20, 22; Tony Aruza, 23; Lafi, 24; Roy Morsch/zefa, 25. *SuperStock:* age footstock, 10; Comstock, 11.

Printed in Malaysia
1 3 5 6 4 2

CONTENTS

The sky is most often blue, but it can be any number of colors. It depends on the position of the Sun and the Moon.

Riding the Wave of Light

Light is all around you. It comes in so many different forms—bright light, dim light, red light, blue light. On a clear day you can see sunlight. Then when the Sun goes down, the sky often glows with beautiful moonlight.

But what is light exactly? It is simply a beam of **energy** moving through space at a great speed. The beam is actually in the form of a **wave.** It is shaped like a wiggly line that moves up and down, up and down. The distance between two peaks on this wiggly line is called a **wavelength.** But light travels so fast that you cannot see its shape or its many waves.

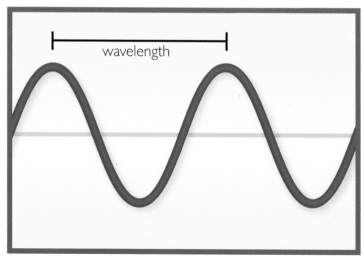

Light is actually energy moving in the form of a wave. The distance between two peaks is known as the wavelength.

5

Riding this wave of energy are billions of tiny particles called **photons.** They are bits of light that are created by **atoms.** An atom is like a building block. Everything is made up of atoms—even you. They are so tiny that you cannot see them without a powerful microscope.

The center of an atom is called the **core.** Moving around the core are **electrons.** The paths that the electrons follow as they circle the core are called **orbits.** When an atom is filled with energy, the electrons leave their normal orbits. They move out and away from the atom. Eventually they fall back into their normal orbits. When they do, they create a small amount of energy in the form of a photon. When millions

Every atom has a core. Electrons move around that core. Everything you can touch and feel is made up of billions of tiny atoms.

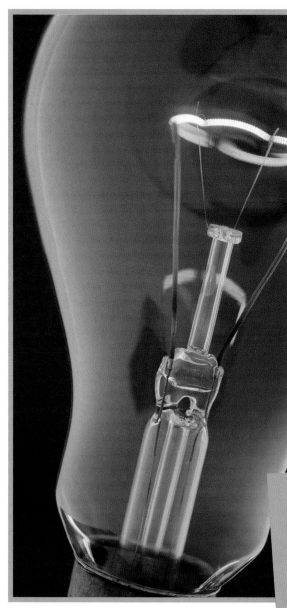

Light is produced by heat, which is why a lightbulb often gets too hot to touch.

of photons travel together in a wave, they create a beam of light.

All the light you see around you comes from a source of heat. That is why a lightbulb gets hot when it is left on. The bulb's **filament** (the thin wire inside it) heats up because electricity is flowing through it. It then sends out photons, making the bulb hot, too. The photons travel through the air and light up a room.

Now I Know!

In what form or shape does light travel through space?

As a wave.

Our eyes can pick up thousands of colors. But there are many more that we cannot see.

Colors of the Rainbow

Look around you. How many different colors are there? Ten? Twenty? A hundred? The answer is actually thousands. But if you tried to count all of them, you wouldn't even come close to that number. How can that be?

Most colors cannot be noticed by the human eye. The only colors we can see are those in the **visible spectrum.**

Colors are created by light waves that have different wavelengths. Light with the longest wavelength in the visible spectrum is seen as red. Light with the shortest wavelength is seen as violet or

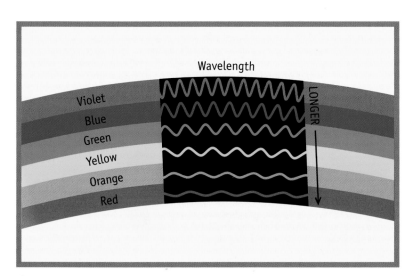

Colors we can see are part of what is called the visible spectrum. Colors we cannot see have wavelengths either too large or too small for us to detect.

purple. Between them are all the other main colors we are able to pick out: orange, yellow, green, blue, and indigo (a purple-blue).

You may have drawn pictures of the Sun, and you probably used the color yellow. But does the Sun really look yellow? No. It is actually closer to white. The white light coming from the Sun is a blend of many colors. If you mix

The Sun and its light often appear to be white, not yellow.

together all the colors of light in the visible spectrum, you get white. That is why a beam of light shining through a glass of water casts rainbow-colored shapes on a wall. The water splits the white beam into the separate colors of light that make up the visible spectrum.

Now I Know!

In the visible spectrum, does red light have the longest or the shortest wavelengths?

The longest.

From white light comes all the colors of the rainbow.

The atmosphere is a mixture of
gases that protect the Earth.

The Air up There

Our planet is surrounded by gases. They form a kind of shell called the **atmosphere.** Without the atmosphere, we would not be able to survive. It keeps in heat while blocking out the cold of outer space. It also protects the Earth from the harmful rays of outer space.

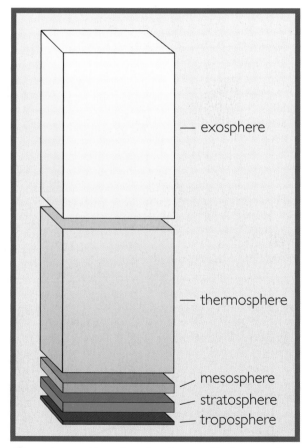

— exosphere

— thermosphere

— mesosphere
— stratosphere
— troposphere

Our atmosphere has five layers. Each one does something different to keep the Earth safe.

The atmosphere has five different layers. The first layer is called the troposphere. This is the part directly above us. It is where weather occurs, such as rainstorms, lightning, and snowfall.

Above the troposphere is the stratosphere. This is where the ozone layer is

13

The ozone layer, which is part of the stratosphere, helps to protect the Earth from harmful rays.

found. It is a band of gas that keeps the Earth safe from most of the **ultraviolet light** that is sent out by the Sun. The ozone layer **absorbs** this harmful light so that it does not reach us.

Next is the mesosphere. It is a very important layer. Millions of meteors and other bits of "space junk" burn up there before they have a chance to reach the Earth.

Above the mesosphere is the thermosphere. Radio signals can bounce off this layer. That is why certain radio signals can be heard hundreds of miles away. They travel up until they bounce off the "ceiling" of the thermosphere at

The mesosphere helps keep harmful objects such as meteors from reaching the Earth's surface. Thousands of meteors pass by the Earth every day.

Clouds are usually only found in the troposphere. This first layer of the atmosphere is where weather, like snow or rain, occurs as well.

an angle. Then they come back to Earth again, where they can sometimes be picked up far away.

Finally, there is the exosphere. This is the last layer of the atmosphere before outer space. The exosphere thins out, until it disappears.

About 78 percent of the gas in the atmosphere is nitrogen. Another 21 percent is oxygen. The remaining 1 percent is a mixture of things. Other gases join with water vapor. Bits of dust and soot from pollution and volcanic eruptions are also found in the air.

Sunlight needs to travel about 93 million miles (150 million kilometers) to reach us, a journey it makes in a little more than eight minutes.

Journey from the Sun

Sunlight travels at great speeds. The distance from the Sun to the Earth is roughly 93 million miles (150 million kilometers). That may seem far. But it actually does not take long for light to reach us—a little more than eight minutes.

Sunlight does not pass directly, or in a straight line, from the Sun to the Earth. It must first travel through the atmosphere's many layers. Many things happen to sunlight when it travels through the atmosphere.

Sunlight has to pass through the atmosphere's many layers. As it does, it goes through several changes.

The atmosphere absorbs some of the heat from the Sun's light before it reaches Earth. The heat that does pass through gives us the warmth we need to survive. Some of this heat leaves the Earth and heads back into space. However, much of

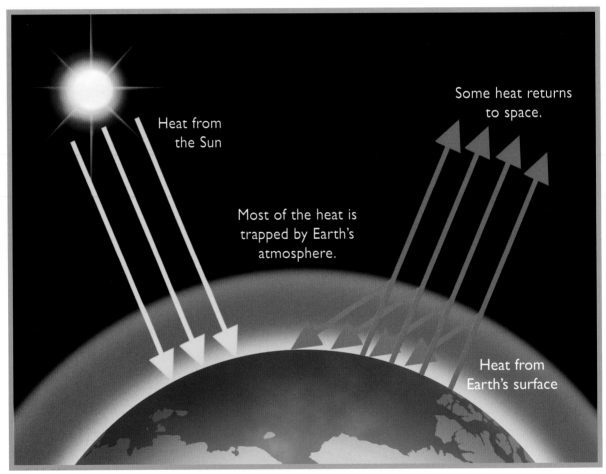

Some heat returns to space.

Heat from the Sun

Most of the heat is trapped by Earth's atmosphere.

Heat from Earth's surface

A process called the greenhouse effect helps warm Earth's surface.

Light not only helps us see, but it also helps us grow. Sunlight is a source of Vitamin D, which makes bones strong.

it is trapped here, so the surface of the Earth becomes warmer. This process is called the **greenhouse effect.**

The atmosphere also **filters** out the harmful effects of ultraviolet light. Ultraviolet helps create Vitamin D in our bodies, which is good for bone growth. But too much of it can cause skin cancer and eye problems.

As it travels to Earth, light also adds color to the sky. So why is the sky blue and not yellow or green?

Now I Know!

Ultraviolet light helps our bodies make what important vitamin?

Vitamin D.

Sunlight striking the Earth's atmosphere is very
similar to light striking a prism. The light
breaks up and scatters in many directions.

Why Is the Sky Blue?

Imagine yourself outside, holding a handful of pebbles. Now imagine throwing those pebbles hard onto the ground. What would they do? They would bounce up and fly off in many

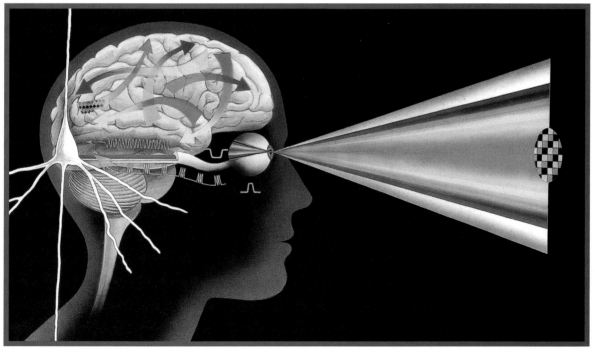

Light enters the eye, which then sends signals to the brain. Blue, red, and green are the easiest colors to pick up. They blend to make all the other colors we see.

23

different directions. Light traveling into the Earth's atmosphere acts in much the same way.

What makes the sky appear to be blue is a process called **scattering.** When the light of the Sun reaches our atmosphere, it slams into the atmosphere's tiny particles. The different colors in the sunlight are then broken up and sent off in different directions. The colors with shorter wavelengths scatter over a larger area than the colors with longer wavelengths. The color that is scattered the most is blue. So, when you look at the sky, that is the color you see. Violet wavelengths are even shorter than blue ones. But our atmosphere absorbs a greater amount of violet than blue. So the blue comes through as the strongest color.

Also, it is easier for our eyes to see blue than violet. There are tiny parts of our eyes called **cones.** There

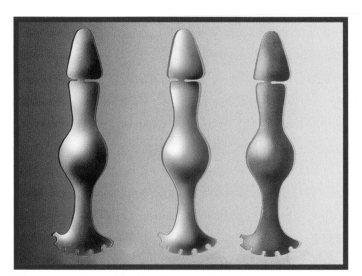

There are three kinds of cones found in your eyes. One picks up blues, another greens, and another reds.

are three types of cones—those that see red, green, and blue. When the cones work together, they can detect all the colors in the visible spectrum. But those three basic colors are still the easiest for us to see. That is why a clear sky can take on such a deep, rich shade of blue. Our eyes absorb it easily.

But if the sky is usually blue, why is it often orange or red at sunset? As the Earth turns, the Sun moves farther away from

The sky is usually blue, but not always. Sometimes a rosy glow can be seen at sunset.

the point at which you are standing. That means sunlight has to travel farther to get to that same point. It must also travel through a thicker layer of atmosphere. By the time the light reaches your eyes, the shorter blue wavelengths are spread out even more and scattered away. That leaves the longer wavelengths of reds, oranges, and yellows. But by the next day, a blue sky is bound to return.

 Activity

Here's how to see the effects of scattering in your own home.

What You Will Need
a small glass fish tank (5 gallon or 19 liter size is best)
water
a flashlight
2 cups milk

What to Do
Fill the tank with water until it is about three-quarters full. Turn on the flashlight and shine it through the tank from one of the shorter ends, so the beam travels the length of the tank. Try to look at the beam from the front, from the back, and from the other end of the tank as well. It is not easy to see it, right? You may notice some bits of dust or other things floating around, but not much else. That is because there is really nothing in the water blocking the path of the beam.

Now pour 1 cup of the milk into the tank, stir, and shine the beam again from the same places. Notice anything different? From the longer sides, the beam will take on a bluish color; and from the far ends, a yellowish or orange color. That is because the tiny particles in the milk are scattering the light beam. As with sunlight entering the Earth's atmosphere, the blues (having shorter wavelengths) are being scattered first, while the oranges and yellows (having longer wavelengths) keep moving along their path. So, you see orange and yellow from the far ends of the tank.

Add the second cup of milk and stir. Both the blues (from the long sides of the tank) and the oranges and yellows (from the far ends) should appear much richer and deeper.

 Glossary

absorb—To take in or draw in.

atmosphere—The collection of gases and dust particles that form a protective shell around the Earth.

atom—The most basic particle of matter. Everything you can touch and feel, for example, is made up of atoms.

cone—An organ inside the human eye that allows us to see colors.

core—The material that makes up the center of an atom.

electron—The part of an atom that has a negative charge.

energy—Power.

filament—The thin wire inside an ordinary lightbulb that glows when the bulb is on.

filter—To bar or stop something from passing through.

greenhouse effect—The way that the Earth's atmosphere traps some of the heat sent from the Sun.

orbit—The path an electron follows while moving around the core of an atom.

photon—A small packet of energy given off by an electron when, after being forced out of its natural orbit, it then falls back into that orbit.

scattering—The way that the Sun's light strikes the Earth's atmosphere and is then broken up into various wavelengths, which create different kinds of light waves.

ultraviolet light—A form of light with a short wavelength. It is invisible to the naked eye and dangerous to humans when they are exposed to it in large amounts or over long periods of time.

visible spectrum—The light that can be seen by the human eye without help from any machine.

wave—Energy that light particles travel along.

wavelength—The distance between two peaks in a wave of energy.

 Find Out More

BOOKS

Fowler, Allan. *All the Colors of the Rainbow*. New York: Children's Press, 1999.

Fullick, Ann. *Seeing Things: Light*. Chicago: Heinemann, 2004.

Hamilton, Gina. *Light: Prisms, Rainbows, and Colors*. Austin, TX: Raintree Steck-Vaughn, 2003.

Lilly, Melinda, and Scott Thompson. *Colors*. Vero Beach, FL: Rourke, 2003.

Nadeau, Isaac. *Water in the Atmosphere*. New York: PowerKids Press, 2003.

Parker, Steve. *Light*. Broomall, PA: Chelsea House, 2004.

Rea, Thelma. *I Wonder Why the Sky Is Blue?* New York: Rosen, 2002.

Tocci, Salvadore. *Experiments with Colors*. New York: Children's Press, 2003.

Trumbauer, Lisa. *All about Light*. New York: Children's Press, 2004.

WEB SITES

http://www.colormatters.com/
Everything you ever wanted to know about color and more!

http://www.extremescience.com
All the areas of science you can imagine, explained in a way you can understand.

http://www.earthsky.com/kids
A really cool science and nature site. Features activities, podcasts, information about a series of "Earth & Sky" radio shows, and answers to common science questions.

http://www.howstuffworks.com/question39.htm
This link brings you right to the page about why the sky is blue. But you should also bookmark the home page, too—it is one of the best all-around sites for young and curious minds.

# Index

Page numbers for illustrations are in **boldface.**